S0-CWV-166

Published by:
Open Pages Publishing
P. O. Box 420788
Houston, Texas 77242
http://www.openpagespublishing.com
Orders: goodstory@openpagespublishing.com

Design and illustration by Barry Gremillion

Text typeface: Bulmer
Illustration medium: ink and watercolor

Although the author and publisher have made every effort to ensure the accuracy and completeness of information contained in this book, we assume no responsibility for errors, inaccuracies, omissions, or any inconsistency herein. Any slight of people places or organizations are unintentional.

First Printing 2006

ISBN 0-9785937-1-5

Publisher's Cataloging-in-Publication
(Provided by Quality Book, Inc.)

Alberti, Frances.
Finding Rover : a true Hurricane Katrina story / by
Frances Alberti ; illustrations by Barry Gremillion.
p. cm.
SUMMARY: A real life adventure story that takes place
in New Orleans during the flooding that occurred after
Hurricane Katrina in August 2005. An older man saves the
lives of two neighbors and his dog Rover.
Audience: Ages 8-12.
ISBN 0-9785937-1-5

1. Alberti, Bobby (Robert)--Juvenile literature.
2. Hurricane Katrina, 2005--Juvenile literature. 3. Dogs--
Juvenile literature. 4. Heroes--Louisiana--New Orleans
--Juvenile literature. 5. Disaster victims--Louisiana--
New Orleans--Juvenile literature. 6. Rescue work--
Louisiana--New Orleans--Juvenile literature. 7. New
Orleans (La.)--Juvenile literature. [1. Alberti, Bobby
(Robert) 2. Dogs. 3. Hurricane Katrina, 2005.
4. Hurricanes. 5. Floods. 6. Heroes. 7. Animal
heroes. 8. New Orleans (La.)] I. Gremillion, Barry.
II. Title. III. Title: True Hurricane Katrina story.

HV636 2005 .L8A43 2006   976.3'35064
QBI06-600254

Acknowledgements

I would like to thank Dick Weiss for his help in editing this book. His wisdom and knowledge of the industry were invaluable to me. His kindness and generosity will never be forgotten. Barry Gremillion for his patience and professionalism under what seemed like an impossible deadline. His wonderful illustrations bring the story to life with such heart and detail it will draw you into the experience on a deep, personal level. Mary Lou Fehr for being one of the first to suggest that I write a children's book of my brother's incredible story. As others confirmed this idea, it became planted in my heart to do so. Thank you for the encouragement. Lynn Manimtim for volunteering her personal time to produce my website. Debbie Markley and Maria Prestigomo for volunteering their proofreading expertise. Last, but certainly not least, for the love and support of my friends and family during this overwhelming endeavor: my sisters Joyce Newman and Nancy Moser; my brother-in-law Pete Newman for always coming to the rescue; my brother-in-law Bob Moser for opening his home to my brother Bobby until he is well again and can re-build his home; my dearest friends Ann Vincent, Townley Stanwood, and Brenda Butcher who are always there when I need them; Carrie Romero who has been a blessing and a dear friend to Bobby and our family for many years.

Author's Note

The purpose of this book is to tell a story of adventure; how 3 people and a dog survived a major disaster. Although based on a true story, the events and characters have been embellished to add drama and interest. The dialog is not always the exact quotes or actual words of the characters nor are they meant to represent anyone's actual words or actions or to resemble or depict actual persons living or dead. The story was developed and enhanced based on an eyewitness account told by one of the characters to the author. Every effort has been made to be sensitive to the nature of the story and to use creative license based on the remembrance of the main character.

*To Bobby, Rover and
all the families who have
suffered from the aftermath
of Hurricane Katrina.
May you all find
your way back home.*

Rover's paw print

Contents

Finding Rover

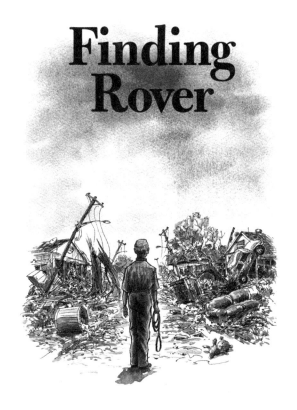

OPEN PAGES PUBLISHING • HOUSTON, TEXAS

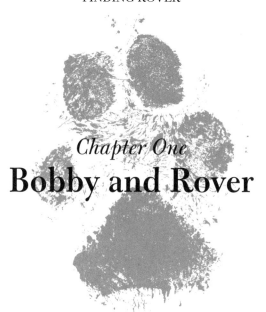

Chapter One
Bobby and Rover

Once, not long ago, in a city called New Orleans, lived a man named Bobby. Bobby grew up with three younger sisters named Nancy, Fran and Joyce, and a younger brother named Dudley. They grew up in an area of New Orleans called the Ninth Ward. As children they loved playing together. They all loved animals. Their mom, Josephine, always had parakeets. Dudley, Bobby's younger brother, had hamsters, homing pigeons and even a baby alligator. Nancy and Fran liked small dogs and had a poodle named Jacques, along with other poodles and schnauzers throughout the years. But Bobby loved large dogs and, from childhood to adulthood, he had dogs named Rex, Jeff and Bull – who were all German shepherds; Shalimar and

Prince, who were Dobermans; and his current and favorite dog, Rover, a Lab-Dalmatian mix.

Bobby – a small, thin, older man with fair skin and blue eyes – lived in a little white house with doors that were trimmed in green. In the front of the house was an iron-rail porch with a green bench. This bench held spe-

cial sentimental value for Bobby. It was where he and his mother would sit for hours just talking and passing the time. Bobby's mother passed away a few years ago, and now it was just Bobby and Rover.

Rover was Bobby's very best friend. He was a large black dog with white on the tips of his back paws and a distinctive black mark on the white hair on his chest. At 80 pounds, Rover weighed almost as much as Bobby.

Every night, the two of them ate dinner together and played. When it was time for bed, Bobby set a timer on his television to wake him for work in the morning.

Rover was a very smart dog. Each morning, when Bobby's television automatically came on, Rover knew it was time for breakfast. Wagging his tail, he would go to the bedroom and poke Bobby with his nose to wake him up. Bobby always looked forward to Rover's greeting each morning.

After they finished eating a delicious breakfast, Rover would go to the coffee table, pick up his leash and take it to Bobby for his morning walk. Rover and Bobby were very happy together. They had all they needed – each other.

During the day, while Bobby was at work, Rover stayed in the yard and played. Sometimes he chased birds and, on other days, he just relaxed in the warmth of the sun. On very hot, humid days, Rover enjoyed dunking his head in his large water bowl to cool off. Sometimes he snapped at flies and bees. Rover looked forward each day to Bobby coming home.

Bobby and Rover lived among interesting neighbors. A musician, who continually played his trumpet, lived next door to Bobby. This fair, thin man, who lived alone, always kept to himself, and was seldom seen by his neighbors. Bobby nicknamed him Toot Toot because all he did was play that trumpet hour after hour, sometimes late into the evening. Since Bobby's bedroom window faced Toot Toot's window, there were many nights he was unable to sleep until the playing stopped.

In the house beside Toot Toot lived a lady named Emily – a kind and friendly lady with shoulder-length brown hair, who worked for the Post Office and lived with her elderly parents. Bobby, Emily and Toot Toot led happy and mostly uneventful lives. But all that changed one day with a weather report: A hurricane named Katrina was bearing down on New Orleans with wind speeds topping 150 miles an hour. Weathermen predicted that Hurricane Katrina could be the worst storm the city had ever seen. The mayor and the police told residents they needed to leave, and thousands did, including Bobby's brother Dudley and his sister, Nancy, who lived elsewhere in the city.

Dudley and Nancy begged Bobby to leave, but Bobby was very stubborn and didn't always listen to his family's advice. Bobby had never left for all the other hurricanes that had struck near New Orleans and he had always been safe. He decided that he and Rover were going to stay.

Dudley, Bobby's younger brother, called Bobby before he left and said, "I'm leaving a life jacket for you on my back patio if you want to come and get it." He loved Bobby very much, but, in his anger and desire to scare him into leaving, he told Bobby, "You're a dead man." Bobby was hurt more than frightened by his brother's remark.

On the day before the hurricane arrived, Bobby heard an inner voice say, "You'd better go and get that life jacket," and so he did. Bobby didn't know how to swim and neither did his neighbors Toot Toot and Emily.

Early the next day, one of Bobby's sisters, Fran, who lived in Houston, called to tell her brother that she loved him and that she would be praying for him. "I'm going to do everything I can to live," he told Fran. He mentioned that he had picked up Dudley's life jacket.

In the days that followed, Fran told her family, "I know Bobby's safe. He has a life jacket and he's too stubborn to die. Besides, I know the Lord will keep him safe. I have many people praying for him." She knew in her heart that God would protect her brother and bring him home.

Chapter Two
Dog Paddling

Just after midnight on August 29, 2005, Hurricane Katrina pounded the streets of New Orleans. The heavy rain and howling winds battered and shook the windows and doors of homes. Large trees snapped like tiny twigs and wooden fences toppled to the ground. Power lines were bent and electrical wires snapped, leaving much of the city in utter darkness. The levees began to break, allowing massive amounts of water to pour into the city, quickly turning streets into rushing rivers.

As the winds howled that morning, Bobby called his neighbor Emily to see if she was okay. Emily's parents had evacuated and she was weathering the storm all alone. Talking on the phone, Bobby and Emily could not believe what they were seeing as they looked out their windows and discussed the devastation. Emily sadly told Bobby that a huge tree had fallen on her car and crushed it. Bobby reported that a large tree had also fallen in his yard. It had landed across his driveway. His wooden fence had also fallen down.

Suddenly the power went out, and Emily and Bobby lost communication. Bobby anxiously looked out the window all night long and was afraid to go to sleep. Each time Bobby rose to take a peek, Rover would follow him to the door with his tail hanging.

The worst part of the storm had passed before dawn – or so it seemed. The streets in Bobby's neighborhood were a little flooded and there were broken limbs and trees everywhere. But Bobby and Rover were safe. "It looks like we made it, Rover!" Bobby exclaimed as he reached to pat Rover on the head. Rover, who had curled up against Bobby's leg with his paws covering his ears, quickly sprang to his feet, tail wagging at the joyful sound in Bobby's voice.

Believing the worst of the storm was over, Bobby decided to go to bed. He was exhausted from staying up all night watching the storm. But, before he did, something told him to look out the door one more time. Since it was still dark, Bobby couldn't see very well. He thought he saw water at the foot of the porch steps. He rubbed his eyes in disbelief thinking he was seeing things. Bobby's heart began to pound rapidly as he watched the water continue to rise to the bottom step of the front porch. He swiftly turned to Rover and yelled "Rover, it looks like we're going for a swim!" Rover, sensing that something was wrong, barked loudly and ran to Bobby's side.

Bobby rushed to the kitchen table, grabbed the life jacket, along with some food cans, bottled water and a can opener. He placed a few cans of dog food and bottled water in a plastic garbage bag. By this time, the water had risen to the top step. "Come on, Rover," Bobby called.

Rover, who followed Bobby everywhere, was frightened and whined loudly as he obediently followed him. The water now stood at Bobby's waist as he stepped from the porch. Rover, with his tail hanging, quickly leaped into the water right behind Bobby.

When Bobby saw the rushing water and fallen power lines, he knew that if he and Rover tried to go into the street they would be swept away and drowned – or electrocuted by a fallen power line.

"Looks like we have to go around the back, Rover. Come on, boy! We've got to help Emily!"

As Bobby waded through the rising water, Rover dog-paddled beside him, softly moaning. They swam to the backyard and went over two fences that had been bent over enough for them to pull themselves over to the other side. But, as they did so, the garbage bag with Rover's food caught on the fence and tore. Bobby frowned as he watched everything sink into the dirty, brown, murky water. It was too late to retrieve his supplies, so he continued to press on.

When they got to Emily's house, Bobby banged very hard on the back door and yelled her name. It took Emily awhile to come to the door and, when she did, Bobby said, "We have to get out of here and get to that house over there."

Bobby pointed to the house next to his with the flat roof. He knew they would have a better chance of surviving there. Bobby's roof, as were most roofs in the neighborhood, was peaked, and he figured they might not be able to hold on very long on a slanted roof.

Emily was frightened and hesitant to go out into the flooded streets, saying, "I can't swim!"

"Do you have a life jacket or something to float on?" Bobby asked.

"I have a floatie" she nervously replied. Emily had a light plastic pool "floatie" with ruffles — the kind you buy for 99 cents at a drugstore. Bobby knew it wasn't strong enough to support Emily in the water for long, so he decided to stay very close to her at all times.

As they waded past Toot Toot's house, they saw him at the back door and encouraged him to come along.

"What are you going to do?" Toot Toot asked.

"I don't know what you're going to do, but we're going to get on that house next to mine with the flat roof. You have to make your move now or we're all going to drown." Bobby called out.

Toot Toot replied, "I can't swim and I don't have a life jacket!" As it turned out, Rover was the only one of the bunch who could swim.

Bobby pointed to nearby fallen trees. "You see those trees and branches, I'll help you grab onto them," Bobby told Toot Toot and Emily.

Emily and Toot Toot quickly pulled themselves from tree to tree. The smelly, murky water swirled all around them. Emily was careful not to catch her plastic floatie on wood or floating debris. Toot Toot followed close behind her, clinging to each branch. Bobby made sure he kept his distance by staying on the other side of the branches. He was afraid that if Toot Toot slipped he might get pulled underwater with him.

Once they made it to Bobby's porch across from the flat-roofed house, Bobby told Emily and Toot Toot to go inside his house since the water was not yet inside. He tried to get Rover to stay with Emily and Toot Toot, too, but Rover was determined to stay at Bobby's side.

As Bobby left, Toot Toot called out to him, "Where are you going?"

"I'm going to swim over to my garage and get the aluminum ladder to place against my neighbor's house so we can climb up to the flat roof," Bobby responded.

As Bobby turned and swam toward the garage, he noticed that Rover was swimming behind him – but he was slowing down and breathing heavily. Bobby knew he would have to work quickly or Rover would be too tired to make it to safety.

Bobby found the ladder and dragged it through the water to the house next door. He propped the ladder up against the side of the house, and then yelled to Emily, "All you have to do is float over here and get on the roof. Do you think you can do it"?

Emily nodded and, with her floatie, jumped off Bobby's porch into the foul-smelling water once again. She waded across the yard near the large fallen tree which kept her from being snatched away by the vicious waters.

Covered in canal sludge from the filthy water, Emily handed Bobby the floatie before grabbing the ladder and pulling herself up to the roof.

"Now when you get to the roof, hold on to the ladder and, whatever you do, don't let it go!" Bobby commanded. "If you do, we won't all be able to get up to the roof."

Emily held on tight to the ladder and Bobby called to Toot Toot. "Now it's your turn."

Bobby swam over to Toot Toot and gave him Emily's floatie. Toot Toot was scared and yelled, "I can't do it! Give me your life jacket."

"Are you crazy?" "I'm not giving you my life jacket so I can drown. I'll help you or you can stay here and drown, but make up your mind fast because the water is rising quickly!" Bobby impatiently replied.

Toot Toot put on the floatie, but when he stepped off the porch he lost his footing. He fell into the polluted, brown water and was pulled under. As he popped back up, Bobby yelled to him "Grab on to the tree branch and I'll help you!"

"I can't, I can't!" Toot-Toot screamed.

Bobby tried to encourage him. "If Emily can do it, so can you," Bobby told him.

With Bobby's help, Toot Toot made his way to the ladder and climbed up onto the roof.

With Rover swimming beside him, Bobby then rushed back inside his home for the last time. The water was now over the porch and flowing into the house. He grabbed a gallon of water and a plastic container with Rover's dog food. He placed the food and water on a rubber tire, pulled it over to the ladder and carried it up to the roof.

In the meantime, Rover was still dog paddling and Bobby could see that his dog was now struggling to stay afloat. He tried to get Rover up on the ladder but he was too heavy to lift. Then Bobby spotted a fallen piece of fence within arm's reach and grabbed it. He pushed it against the house and leaned on it so it wouldn't move. Then he tapped on the board and called to Rover, "Come on, boy. Get up! Come on, Rover, jump!"

Rover tried, but slipped back into the murky water, yelping in defeat. Bobby, unwilling to lose his loyal friend, commanded Rover to jump once again. Rover lunged forward and got his front paws on the board. Then Bobby quickly grabbed him by his back end and pushed him up on the board. Rover was so exhausted and frightened that he stood on the board, with his ears down and his tail between his legs, and didn't move.

Relieved that Rover was safe for the moment, Bobby climbed the ladder to join Toot Toot and Emily on the roof. He was tired, scared and very sad. He sat on the edge of the roof with his legs hanging over the side holding on to the 25-foot leash that was still attached to Rover.

As they sat on the roof there was an eerie silence. No wind, birds, bugs or people could be seen or heard except for one man yelling for help in the distance. There was nothing they could do to help him. The deafening silence and haunting voice tugged at Bobby's heart. He turned away from the haunting cry as he watched the water rise to the windows of his house, hoping that help would come soon.

With moist eyes and deep sadness, he watched his house go under water. He had lived in this house with his mother most of his life. She was so happy when she had finished paying for it just two years earlier. Within a few hours, the destruction was complete. Poof! All gone, just like that.

Chapter Three
Rescued

Bobby, Emily and Toot Toot sat on the sun-baked rooftop for just 30 minutes before help arrived – but it seemed like it had been an eternity, when Emily suddenly yelled, "I hear a helicopter"!

Sure enough, a helicopter was flying toward them! The trio stood up, yelled and waved frantically to the helicopter. The Coast Guardsman flying the helicopter signaled to them but indicated he had too many passengers to pick them up. A few minutes later, another helicopter came. As it hovered near the house, a Coast Guardsman came down on a cable.

He dropped in front of Bobby and said, "You're going into the basket first, then him (meaning Toot Toot) and then her." But Bobby refused to leave without Rover and replied, "Not without my dog, I'm not!" The rescuer said, "Okay, man, we'll get your dog."

The man then attached a cable to Rover and he and Bobby pulled Rover up on the roof. Rover was so glad to be at Bobby's side again that he started licking him in the face.

Bobby got into the basket and became a little dizzy as the basket turned in circles in the air. He decided to close his eyes so he wouldn't get sick. Emily held on to Rover as the dog began barking and whining as Bobby was lifted out of his sight. The guardsmen later hoisted Toot Toot and then Emily, with

Rover in her basket, into the helicopter. Rover had willingly gone into the basket with Emily knowing that Bobby was up there somewhere.

As they flew over the city to a school campus that was being used as a shelter for flood victims, they saw houses covered in water as far as the eye could see. They were very sad, yet grateful they were alive.

When they arrived at the shelter, their clothes were still wet and covered with mud and dirty water. They were given bottled water and chocolate chip cookies – the only food the shelter could provide. There was neither running water nor air conditioning and it was very, very hot. Since there was no clean, dry clothing for them, Bobby, Toot Toot and Emily had to sleep in their mud-crusted, wet clothing. And since there were no beds or

blankets, Bobby shared his life jacket with Emily as a pillow. Rover nestled between them with his head on Bobby's leg. They awoke the next morning with sore muscles from sleeping on the hard ground, but with hope for a better day.

It was a better day because Bobby met a man named Bryan. Bryan also had a dog and offered to share his dog food with Rover. Bobby was glad that Rover could get something to eat since he only had had water since he was taken from the rooftop. Rover was so hungry that he quickly gobbled up every bite of food. Afterward, the two dogs played together.

Soon, there was also more food for the people at the shelter. A grocery store not far away had opened its doors to let the people at the shelter take whatever food they wanted. But when Bobby and Rover got to the store, he was shocked at what he saw. Many people simply rushed into the store, pushing, grabbing food, and knocking over shelves. Bobby said to Rover, "Let's get out of here boy, before someone gets hurt!"

Later that evening, some of the same people who had caused trouble in the store became rowdy again. Bobby said to Emily, "We'd better sleep outside. It's not safe in here." So Bobby rolled up his life jacket and he, Rover and Emily bedded down for the night on the hard cement ground once again.

By the next day, the hot and smelly shelter was overcrowded. As Bobby and Emily walked around outside to escape the heat and noise, helicopters started to fly in from everywhere – flocks of them. The people at the shelter were told that everyone had to be moved to a different location because another levee nearby had failed. This was bad news, but, as it turned out, it was even worse than Bobby could imagine.

Chapter Four
Leaving Rover

"Okay, everyone listen!" a Coast Guardsman called out to the people in the shelter. "All of you must be moved immediately to another shelter and no animals will be allowed there. You will have to leave your animals behind. It is no longer safe to remain here."

Bobby could hardly believe what he was hearing. "How can I leave Rover behind after all we've been through?" he thought.

Tears ran down his cheeks as he gave Rover a quick pat on the head. He asked Bryan if he would watch his dog. Bryan replied, "I'll watch him for as long as I can, but I'll have to leave both dogs behind when it's my turn to leave." Then they both exchanged phone numbers and promised to help each other retrieve their dogs. While Rover was playing with another dog, Bobby quickly disappeared around a corner. He didn't want Rover to see him walking away. He couldn't bear to look at him. His heart was broken.

On the helicopter, Bobby began to feel guilty, "Look what you did," he told himself. "You gave up your best friend."

He stared out of the helicopter window in disbelief. Water was everywhere. It covered roof tops and the streets had turned into raging rivers that carried cars, roofs and siding, furniture and garbage in their wake.

Just a few minutes later, Bobby could see Interstate 10, a main highway

leading out of town. Below him, he saw long lines of yellow school buses ready to take evacuees like him to the next shelter. The last time Bobby had been in a school bus was when he was a little boy. Back then, he knew where that yellow school bus was taking him – to school. But not this time.

The Coast Guardsmen wouldn't tell Bobby, Emily or Toot Toot where they were going. They just needed to get on the bus. Bobby was tired, hungry and very sad as he boarded.

As it turned out, Bobby and his fellow passengers were driven to a shelter in Houma, Louisiana, about an hour from New Orleans. At this shelter, they were examined by doctors, given clean clothes and a shower. It felt so good to be clean again. They were even more excited to see hot food ready for them to eat. They got into line and filled their plates and ate every bite.

The building was even air conditioned, and they were given blankets and a pillow. Bobby thought, "You never know how lucky you are until you lose everything you have – the roof over your head and food to eat."

Tired and worn out, Bobby and Emily once again shared the life jacket as a pillow. This night, Bobby was really sad because Rover was not at his side.

In the morning, Bobby and Emily learned that meals were served exactly at 8 a.m., noon and 6 p.m. If you missed a meal, you went hungry until the next meal. At night, everyone had to be back at the shelter by 8 p.m. when the doors were locked for the night. If you were late, you were not allowed back in and had to sleep outside. Bobby and Emily obeyed the rules.

With little to do during the day, everyone shared their stories with each other. Bobby would also go outside and watch the helicopters fly in with more evacuees. Emily walked up to Bobby and said, "I'm going to see if I

can find a way to contact my brother to let him know where I am. Do you want to come?"

Bobby nodded. He needed to let his sister in Texas know he was okay. But he and Emily had a hard time getting a phone line out of the hurricane-damaged area.

The next day Bobby went to a pay phone across the street from the shelter. He would try and try but the lines were always busy and he could never get through. Bobby saw a man who was handing out bottled water. He came up to Bobby and said, " I'm Forrest and I come down here everyday to give people water and see if I can help them with anything. Do you need anything?"

"I have my sister's phone number and I can't get through," Bobby said. "If I give it to you would you keep trying for me? I have to get back to the shelter before they close the doors at 8 p.m."

Forrest promised, "Sure man I'll be glad to call your sister. I'll keep calling her until I get her."

Bobby gave him the number. He thought, "I bet he doesn't call" and never thought about it again. Bobby had seen a lot of promises broken in his life and he didn't have much hope that this promise would be kept either.

When Bobby returned to the shelter, he noticed a man visiting with everyone. When the man walked up, Bobby asked him, "What's your story man?" The man replied, what do you mean, what's my story? Bobby replied, everyone is telling a story about how they escaped the flood?" So, what's yours?"

The man told Bobby that he was a pastor. "I'm just walking around to find out how I can help people and to pray for them. Can I help you with something?" What do you need?"

Bobby replied, "You would be doing me a big favor if you would call my sister in Texas. My family doesn't know whether I'm alive or dead or where I am. They haven't heard from me in four days."

The pastor replied, "I would be glad to call your sister and will keep trying until I get her, I promise."

He took the phone number from Bobby and left. Bobby thought, "I wonder if he really will try to call."

He no longer had faith in promises; not even the promise of a pastor. You see, Bobby didn't realize how God was reaching out, once again, through others to help him. Nor did he know the miracles that were yet in store for him.

Chapter Five
Promises Kept

Bobby soon learned that people do keep their promises. Five days after the hurricane, Bobby's sister, Joyce, received phone calls from the pastor and another man who had offered to help. Joyce was so excited to hear that Bobby was alive that she began to cry.

She called her sister Fran, saying, "Frances, they've found Bobby and he's okay. He's in Houma, Louisiana. Call me right away!" Unfortunately, Fran did not get home and hear the message until three hours later. When Fran finally got the message she called Joyce and they cried and laughed together over the good news. Deep in their hearts, Fran and Joyce had known that somehow Bobby would make it home.

Remember Nancy, Bobby's sister who left with her husband to escape the hurricane? Well, the night before the hurricane hit, she was packing to leave and started feeling very, very sick. Her husband Bob rushed her to the emergency room and the doctors made her well enough to travel. By the time they got home, the hurricane was very close – just a day away. Since the weather was bad, they could not make it to Houston. They only got as far as a city called Gonzales, Louisiana, where Bob's aunt lived. This was no accident. It was just as God had planned it; they were only 90 minutes from the shelter where Bobby was staying.

When Nancy learned where Bobby was, she and her husband immediately set out to get her brother so he wouldn't have to stay in a shelter another night. When they arrived at the shelter it was almost midnight. A policeman approached their car and said, "No one is allowed on the streets after 8 p.m., you'll have to leave." Nancy tried to explain why they were there, but the man said, "I'm sorry miss, that's the rules."

Determined to get Bobby anyway, they drove around the back of the building and Nancy's husband told her to stay in the car and he would get Bobby. It seemed like forever, but finally Bobby came around the corner holding a brown paper sack.

Nancy bolted out of the car and cried out, "You made it, you made it. You look real good!" Although Bobby's face was burned and peeling he looked healthy. Nancy noticed that Bobby was very thin and the clothes he received at the shelter just hung on his body. A belt was holding up pants that were twice his size, but at least they were clean.

Bobby told them about how he had to leave Rover behind. It was a story he would tell many times over – a story that would take him on another journey, for God had another surprise in store for Bobby.

Chapter Six
Haunting Memories

The following day, Bobby, Nancy and her husband Bob drove to Fran's place in Houston, Texas. When Fran opened the door, Bobby broke down crying and said, "I made it." Once again Bobby told his story, this time to his sisters Fran and Joyce. After Bobby spent some time talking with his sisters and relaxing, Bobby and his family drove to Bellville, Texas to stay with his sister Joyce and her husband Pete until Bobby could return home to Louisiana.

Bellville is a small town near rolling green hills and pastures with big cows and horses. The town square is surrounded by restaurants, a pharmacy, and antique and craft stores. Like most small towns, it is quaint and everyone seems to know each other. The people are warm and friendly.

Although Bobby had his family around him now, he often sat alone for many hours on the front porch, staring into space and not saying a word. Often he would get up and take long walks, not telling anyone where he was going or when he would be back. He thought about whether Rover had survived and, if he had, what each day was like for him.

At first, Bobby's family was very worried about all the time he spent alone, but they came to understand that he needed this time alone to heal.

One day, Bobby and his sister Nancy decided to have breakfast at

Newman's Bakery – a small restaurant and bakery where people could hang out and talk. Bobby sat down and started talking to a few people. When he began to tell his story, he left tears in the eyes of many. He enjoyed going to Newman's Bakery since he spent many lonely hours waiting for his family to come home from their jobs. On his long walks during the day, he would sometimes go in to the restaurant for coffee and donuts and would tell his story once again. Before long, almost everyone in town knew the story about Joyce's brother Bobby.

As Bobby sat on the patio of his sister's home, he was haunted by the memories of Rover, and how Rover would wake him up in the mornings before the hurricane. He missed that daily routine. He kept thinking, "Why did you leave that dog? How could you have left that dog?" He told his sisters, "I don't care about the house, I don't care about anything. I just want my dog."

Fran told Bobby, "We're going to find your dog. I know we are."

But Bobby wondered if he would ever see Rover again.

Chapter Seven
Finding Rover

To help Bobby find Rover, Fran placed ads on the Internet and spent hours each day searching through pictures and descriptions of missing dogs. It was now three weeks since Bobby had left Rover behind. Fran heard that thousands of rescued dogs were being taken to a shelter in Gonzales, Louisiana. One Saturday, she told Bobby, "Let's go and see if Rover is in Gonzales."

With high hopes, they packed the car with a leash, water, dog food and towels and blankets to feed and wash Rover when they found him. Six hours later, they arrived in Gonzales and began to look in hundreds of cages for Rover's face, but with no luck. The ride home seemed a lot longer than six hours with Bobby and Fran hardly exchanging a word. Bobby now had no hope that he would find Rover again.

But Fran didn't give up. On Saturday, September 24, Fran took another look at the Pet Harbor Web site where she had placed an ad for Rover. Everyone was watching television as Bobby sat alone outside on the front porch once again. Fran told Nancy and Joyce, "I'm going to look for Rover again on this Web site. Do you want to look with me?"

Nancy and Joyce followed Fran to the computer to look at the dogs. Suddenly, Nancy pointed to one of the photos. "That's Rover!"

"Are you sure?" Fran asked.

"Yes, I'm sure.

"Go get Bobby and bring him in here," Fran said.

Bobby came in dragging his feet, but when he saw the picture of Rover, he perked up. He couldn't believe his eyes and said, "That's my dog!"

"Are you sure it's Rover?" Fran asked. A notation said that he was at the Gonzales center where Bobby and Fran had been just days before.

Bobby said, "I oughtta know my own dog. That's Rover! That's him! He has white on his chest with a little black spot and white on the tips of his back paws. That's definitely him."

Bobby didn't like showing too much emotion, but Fran, Joyce and Nancy got very excited. It was the best day ever in a long time for Bobby and his family. God showed Bobby that he was there for him once again. Just like Fran knew God would.

This time, they had a picture and a number to take with them when they went back to Gonzales to pick up Rover. Bobby's sisters Joyce, Nancy and Fran were so excited that they all decided to drive to Louisiana with Bobby to get Rover.

There was only one problem: Hurricane Rita had passed through Houston just two days before. Millions of people had left Houston in bumper-to-bumper traffic, and now they were returning to the city and causing more traffic jams.

On Wednesday, September 28, when it was safe to travel, Fran, Joyce, Nancy and Bobby packed up and left for Gonzales to get Rover. They drove through Beaumont, Texas, and Lake Charles, Louisiana, where Hurricane Rita had hit. There were no gas stations, highway lights or any place to eat or stop. Everything was destroyed. Electric poles were bent or broken in half. Trees were bent like pretzels. Homes were flattened and roofs ripped off. Windows of hotels were blown out, with torn drapes left flapping in the wind. The exits were blocked by the military because streets were still flooded, and rubble and trash were everywhere. It was very sad and upsetting to see the total destruction. Bobby and his sisters had seen enough hurricane damage to last them for a lifetime.

When they arrived at the shelter, Joyce showed the lady at the check-in table the paper with Rover's picture and ID number. But she could not find Rover on her computer list. She said that Rover may not have been entered into the computer yet. She said they could not keep up with the thousands of dogs that were being dropped off after their rescue from the hurricane-flooded streets.

Bobby was dragging his feet with a sad look on his face as he, Fran and Nancy began to look again in the cages.

"We'll never find him," Bobby said.

Fran and Nancy told him he needed to have faith. Bobby just grunted and started walking toward the stalls. It was a hot humid day. They walked along five or six rows of horse stalls with 3-4 cages in each stall. Fans were placed in the stalls to keep the dogs cool from the intense heat. There were hundreds of dogs of all kinds: big dogs, little dogs and many black dogs that looked like Rover.

When they came across a large black dog, Bobby and his sisters would look for white on the back paws and white on the chest with a black spot. Each time it was not Rover, sadness filled Bobby's eyes.

Some of the dogs were too sick to stand up or too sad to get up because they missed their master. Some would moan with a look that said, "Please take me home!" Fran had to hold back tears as she looked at all the lonely and frightened dogs.

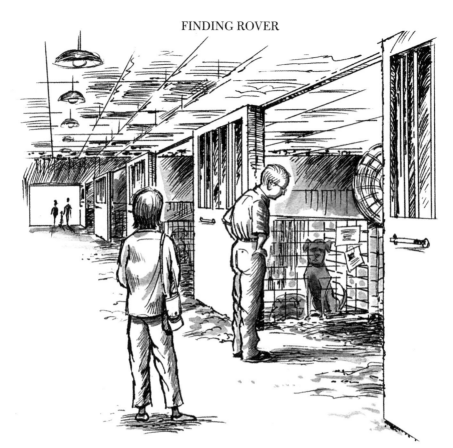

Joyce learned that hundreds of dogs had been moved to other dog shelters in states across the country and that about 100 dogs had been taken to St. Louis, Missouri, the previous Friday. Bobby and his sisters had finished going through every cage without any luck.

One of the volunteers said to look again, because Rover could be getting a bath or being walked. Bobby, Nancy and Fran walked through one more time, but Bobby dragged behind feeling hopeless. It was then that Fran prayed, "Lord, we need divine favor and we need it now."

Her prayer was answered as a lady named Carla, who was on one of the dog rescue teams, walked up and said to Nancy, "Hi, how are you doing. Have you found your dog?"

"No, and we have the picture and ID number that says he should be here," Fran replied. "They told us that hundreds of dogs were sent to shelters across the country. How are we ever going to find our dog?"

Carla replied, "Follow me. I'm going to take you to someone who can find your dog today."

They followed her to a trailer. She knocked on the door and went in while Bobby, Fran and Nancy waited outside. In a few minutes, the trailer door opened and Carla and another woman stepped out.

"This is Sara," Carla said. "She is with the Humane Society of the United States. If anyone can help you, she can." As Bobby and Fran told Sara their story, her eyes became moist. She looked at Fran and said, "We're going to find out where your dog is today. I'm going to give you my personal cell phone number. If I don't call you in three hours, you call me."

It was nearly lunch time, so Bobby and his sisters returned to Aunt Audrey's house in Gonzales to wait for the phone call. Sure enough, Sara called within three hours as promised and told Fran that Rover was in St. Louis. Bobby's dog had been placed in a foster home by the Humane Society of Missouri. She gave Fran the name and number of the person to contact.

Fran called a woman named Pam at the St. Louis Humane Society. Pam told her that Rover was in a foster home. The couple were bringing him back tomorrow because he was sick. "We'd like a vet to look at him and make sure he is well enough to travel before you come and get him," Pam said. "It's probably nothing to worry about. Rover had an infection when he first arrived here, probably from drinking dirty water."

Pam then asked Fran, "Can your brother fly or drive to St. Louis to get Rover?"

"My brother has lost everything," Fran said. "He can't afford to fly right now and is not well enough to drive."

Pam said, "I'll call you tomorrow after talking to my supervisor. In the meantime, Rover will be taken good care of. He is such a sweet dog and everyone loves him."

The next day, Fran and Bobby received a phone call from Pam.

"The Humane Society would like to pay for a hotel and airfare for both you and your brother to come to St. Louis and get Rover," Pam told Fran.

"We are also checking with the airlines to have Rover flown back with you. We would like to know if Bobby would give his story to the press."

Bobby quickly agreed. He was normally a man who didn't like a lot of attention, but he said, "If that's what I have to do to get my dog, okay."

Chapter Eight
Reunion

On Sunday, October 2, Bobby and Fran boarded the plane to St. Louis. When they arrived, a driver hired by the Humane Society took them to their hotel. The hotel and all their meals were paid for by the Humane Society. On their way to the hotel, Fran called Pam, who was to meet them and take them to the shelter to see Rover. When they arrived an hour later, Bobby and Fran were taken to a room to wait while Pam went to get Rover. Although it was only minutes, it seemed like forever.

Then Pam walked into the room with Rover. He began to sniff Bobby for a few seconds as though he couldn't believe it, but was making sure it was him. Then, in an instant, his tail began to wag. He started whining with joy as he jumped on Bobby, knocking him against the wall and licking his face.

"Oh, Rover, I got you back," Bobby said, beaming. "I never thought I would get you back."

Rover was so excited that he kept panting and jumping on Bobby as Bobby held back his tears. Pam decided it would be good to take Rover for a walk in the park across the street to calm him down. Fran followed with her camera in hand, taking pictures of this happy, exciting reunion.

As Bobby held the leash tight, Rover circled him and continued to jump up, licking him in the face. Bobby began to give Rover commands, "Sit,

Rover," "Roll over, Rover," "Down boy, down" – which Rover did with great delight, wanting to please the man he loved and had not seen for over a month.

As they began to walk back to the shelter, Pam told Bobby and Fran that the first interview would be with the St. Louis Post-Dispatch and then with television reporters of three local stations. They were also trying to get them on a network program like the *Today Show* or *Good Morning, America*. She said they had a cake for Rover and invited the Humane Society staff to celebrate Rover's reunion.

When Bobby and Fran returned to the hotel room they had dinner and got ready for bed. Bobby told Fran, "You didn't say it was going to be this big, I just want my dog." "You'll be fine. You've told your story many times. You can do it," Fran replied.

The next morning, they were brought to the same room at the shelter where Bobby first saw Rover. And again, when Rover was brought into the room, he began to sniff and jump and lick Bobby in the face. Bobby decided to sit in a chair and commanded, "Rover, sit. Down, boy."

Rover, who was a very well-trained dog, was too excited to obey the commands for longer than a second.

The reporter from the *St. Louis Post-Dispatch* entered the room for her interview. Because Rover was so frisky, he was taken back to his cage until the interview was over. News reporters, with cameras and lights, were everywhere. It was like making a movie and Bobby and Rover were the stars for the day.

A reporter and camera man first asked Fran questions about how Rover had been found. Then Bobby and Rover came out and walked over to a decorated table that held a beautiful cake that the Humane Society had made for them. The cake's icing featured a dog made of chocolate with a blue collar, a red tongue hanging out of its mouth, and chocolate and white icing for the eyes. There was a white dog bone trimmed in chocolate with Rover's name on it. Around the sides of the cake were dog bones made of

white icing with chocolate trim.

The cake read, "Happy Reunion, Rover and Bobby." The table was decorated with pretty yellow plates and napkins and colored balloons.

Bobby and Rover were surrounded by reporters and Humane Society employees who applauded as they walked up to the table. Camera flash bulbs were going off and mikes and lights were everywhere as Bobby asked Rover to do tricks for the reporters.

Bobby told his dog, "Look, Rover, you're a movie star."

As Bobby kneeled next to him, Rover tried to reach up to lick the cake. Bobby and Fran, though, gently pulled Rover away from the cake.

When one of the reporters asked Bobby how he felt about leaving Rover behind, Bobby replied, "It was hard to do, but I figured I had to do it quick and get it over with, you know, and that's what I did."

Another reporter asked how Bobby had recognized Rover, with all the thousands of dogs on the Internet. Bobby replied, "On his chest he has a spot, a black spot, and that did it." When asked how he felt now that he had Rover back, Bobby chuckled and said, "I feel good, real good. He's my best friend, and we'll never be separated again."

It was nearly 5 p.m. by the time Bobby and Fran returned to the hotel. Fran turned on the television to see if their story was on. Sure enough, there they were with Rover on three local channels. One of the news stations started the story with a large picture of Bobby and Rover on one side and a large picture of Rover's face on the other which said, "Sole Companion." Another channel started with a poster of Rover that read "Happy Reunion."

The next morning held another surprise. As Bobby and Fran went to have breakfast, they bought a newspaper to look for the article about Rover. Bobby was shocked when he opened the paper. "Rover and I are on the front page! It's kind of weird to see yourself on the front page of a newspaper. I thought it might be a small article somewhere in the middle of the paper."

Fran grabbed the paper and told Bobby to buy three more for the family. It was a great way to start the morning and to get ready for the trip home. Since it was too hot to put Rover in the cargo area of a plane back to Houston, the Humane Society rented a minivan large enough to fit Rover, his dog house and a large bag of food for their long ride home.

On the ride home, Fran would stop driving long enough to let Bobby walk Rover. Whenever Bobby got out of the van, Rover would whine anxiously and look out the van's windows for his friend. Rover, no doubt, remembered the last time Bobby walked away and didn't come back.

In those long four weeks that Rover had been missing, he was cared for by many different people. But Rover was surely confused, lonely and sad not knowing where he would find himself next. Until he was home with Bobby and back into their daily routine, he would not feel safe again.

Bobby and Rover returned to New Orleans three months after

Hurricane Katrina. They now live with Bobby's sister Nancy and her husband, Bob, just a few miles from where Bobby used to live.

On Saturdays, Bobby would put Rover in his car and drive. His sister Nancy said they would not see him again until later in the evening. One day his sister Joyce was talking to Bobby on the phone and said, "Nancy told me on Saturdays you just disappear and don't come home until evening. What do you do all that time?"

Bobby replied, "I just drive around New Orleans and go to my old neighborhood to see if any of my neighbors have returned. You know the green iron bench that mom used to sit on is still there, chained to the railing. She loved to sit outside on that bench. Now, the bench is the only thing left."

"I sit on the bench and think about how things used to be and wonder what tomorrow will bring. I can only take it a day at a time. On my last visit while sitting on the bench I noticed that the grass was beginning to come back."

Bobby realized that he would never know what each new day would bring. But one thing was certain. There would be another day, good or bad. And the grass would grow again.

Photo by the the author

Send this form only

Telephone orders: Call 888-257-0696 toll free.

E-mail orders: goodstory@openpagespublishing.com

Website: http://openpagespublishing.com

Postal Orders: Open Pages Publishing, P. O. Box 420788, Houston, TX 77242

Donations of any amount are welcome to help Bobby and Rover return home..

Please print only

Name:

Address:

City: State: Zip:

Telephone:

Email address:

	U. S. (Domestic)	International
Price $10.95 x _____ No. Ordered=		
Sales Tax (Please add 8.25% for products shipped to Texas)		
Shipping & Handling -1 Book	4.05	5.25
Shipping & Handling Additional Books		
Grand Total		

Shipping by air - Note shipping rates are 2006 U.S.Postal Rates and are subject to change.

U.S.: $4.05 for first book and $2.00 for each additional book.
International: $5.25 for first book and $2.00 for each additional book

Payment: ☐ Check (Payable to *Open Pages Publishing*) *Note: 2 or more books by credit card only.*

☐ Credit Card   ☐ Visa   ☐ MasterCard

Card number

Name on card   Exp. Date:

Signature:

Thank you!